To Suvo & John
with best love
from one author
Ennry Bunher

SECRET SPLENDORS
OF THE CHINESE COURT

QING DYNASTY COSTUME FROM THE CHARLOTTE HILL GRANT COLLECTION

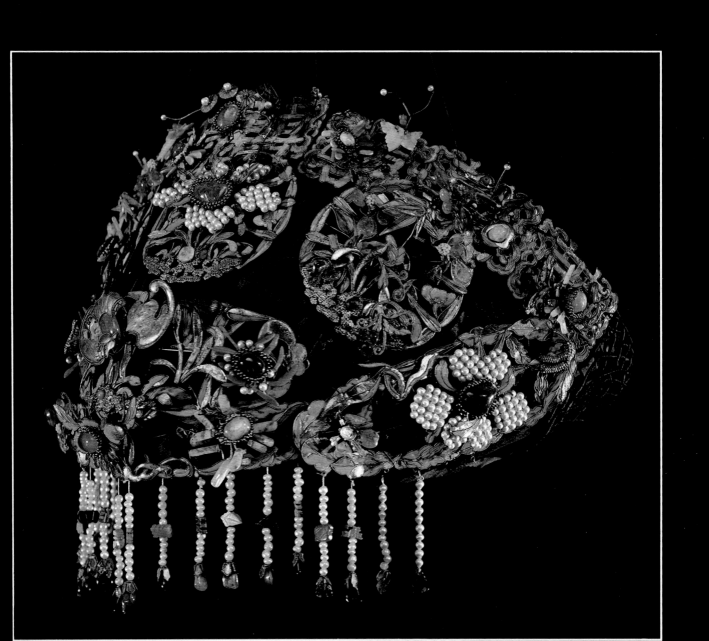

The exhibition is made possible by grants from the Helen K. and Arthur E. Johnson Foundation and the National Endowment for the Arts. The catalog is supported by the Ruth and Vernon Taylor Foundation.

Denver Art Museum
100 West 14th Avenue Parkway
Denver, Colorado 80204

Editors: Marlene Chambers, Carol Rawlings, Margaret Ritchie
Photographers: Lloyd Rule, Richard Baume
Designer: Fred Rainey

Typesetting by Lettergraphics/Denver, Inc.
Lithography by A. B. Hirschfeld Press

All objects illustrated are from the Charlotte Hill Grant Collection except where noted. This catalog uses the pinyin system of romanization of Chinese terms.

Cover: Man's dragon robe, 1750-1775.
Silk brocade. 1977.190

Of this robe, Charlotte Hill Grant wrote:
"This is the only robe in the collection having the four-clawed dragons that were used to designate the rank of the lower order of princes. . . . The four full-faced dragons on the upper part of this robe are several inches larger than corresponding dragons on later robes. They are woven in richly colored bronze-gold thread with effulgent flame-like appendages in the soft blues, reds, and golds and have outlining accents in glowing 'pearl' white. Cumulous clouds and large gracefully designed bats are softly colored—resembling clouds seen at sunset."

Title page: Dragon medallion, 1875-1900.
Gold and silk embroidery on silk satin.
Gift of Mrs. Carroll B. Malone. 1973.378.1

This embroidered medallion is one of a pair displaying the late Qing dynasty tendency to copy Ming styles. With their frontal, five-clawed dragons, the medallions could have been presentation pieces or emblems for a woman's informal coat.

Bride's headdress, 18th/19th century.
Silk, gold wire, jade, pearls, rose quartz, kingfisher feathers.
Gift of Mrs. J. Churchill Owen. 1973.23

TABLE OF CONTENTS

Overleaf: Pocket and ring case, c. 1875. Silk embroidery on silk. 1977.389.1,2

This pocket holds a rectangular box containing 36 carved mother-of-pearl pieces for Fairy Game, said to have been a favorite of Empress Dowager Cixi. The matching ring case was made to hold two archer's rings.

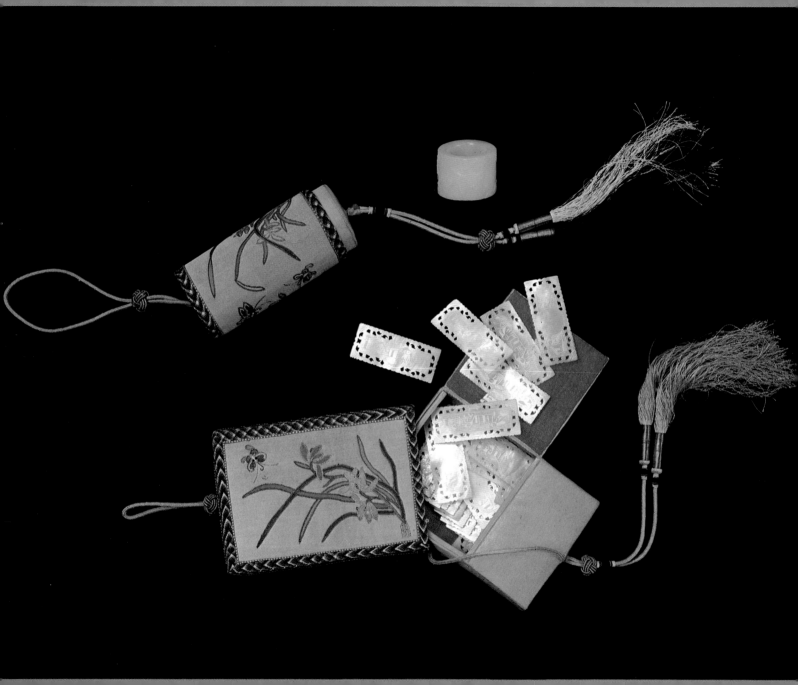

ACKNOWLEDGMENTS

Major exhibitions of this sort could not be organized without the generous support of many contributors. Our particular thanks is owed to the Helen K. and Arthur E. Johnson Foundation and the National Endowment for the Arts for grants which made the exhibition possible. We are equally indebted to the assistance of the Ruth and Vernon Taylor Foundation for the publication of this catalog, which complements and documents the exhibition.

I am also grateful to those whose talents and time have helped make the project a reality. The contributions and support of staff colleagues have been particularly gratifying. Ronald Otsuka, curator of Asian art, shared his expertise in many ways, as well as contributing an informative essay to this catalog. The tedious and time-consuming task of editing was accomplished by Marlene Chambers and her staff. Their patience, professional skill, and wide-ranging knowledge were invaluable. Fred Rainey succeeded in creating a catalog with extraordinary visual impact. Hours behind the lens and in the darkroom resulted in the fine photography credited to Lloyd Rule and his assistant Richard Baume. Their achievement contributed a great deal to the success of this project. The skill and imagination of Jeremy Hillhouse and Amy Metier Brown helped create an exhibition environment that does full justice to

Pocket, c. 1875. Silk embroidery on silk. 1977.380

a sumptuous costume collection. Nancy Roberts, former curatorial assistant, spent many painstaking hours recording the catalog notes of Charlotte Hill Grant. Her dedication simplified the entire project for everyone.

Special mention is in order for Jean Wilson, an intern from the University of Denver, who joined our department when the project was well under way. Her research resulted in educational material utilized in docent training and gallery installation. From Julie Segraves came invaluable information based on two years' research of the collection. This specialized knowledge and her academic training in Chinese art and culture have benefited every aspect of the exhibition. Her enthusiasm animates her essay on court life.

Other authorities have been generous in contributing to the catalog. Emma C. Bunker, former Denver Art Museum research associate and faculty member at Colorado College, brings to life the history and legends of the Manchu conquerors of China. John E. Vollmer, associate curator of the Textile Department at the Royal Ontario Museum, discusses the impact of Manchu clothing traditions on Qing court costume. Major Chinese technical accomplishments in the art of silk production are treated by Dr. Dieter Kuhn, noted scholar and lecturer in the East Asian Department of the Institute of Art History at Heidelberg University. The intricacies of Chinese embroidery are detailed by Elsa S. Williams, prominent authority on ancient and modern needlework and author of many books on the subject.

Last, but by no means least, I gratefully acknowledge the many volunteer hours spent by staff aides who participated in preparation of material for the catalog and exhibition: Toby Bowlby, Anne Theobald, Nancy Iona, Elfriede Von Glinski, Doris Smith, Janis Bente, Lisa Bakewell, Mary Pierce, and Maxine Friedman.

Imelda Gatton DeGraw
Curator of Textiles and Costumes

INTRODUCTION

The Charlotte Hill Grant Collection of costumes and accessories worn at court during the Qing dynasty (1644-1912) includes some 500 objects from the most dazzling period of imperial China. These holdings—the largest single costume collection yet to be given to the Denver Art Museum—were acquired through the gift of James P. Grant and Betty Grant Austin and museum purchase.

Charlotte Grant (1894-1973) arrived in Beijing with her husband, Dr. John B. Grant, and their daughter, Betty, in 1922. There, under the auspices of the International Health Board of the Rockefeller Foundation, Dr. Grant established his reputation as a pioneer and innovator in the field of public health at Beijing Union Medical College. For Dr. Grant, who was born in 1890 in his father's missionary hospital at Ningbo, the assignment was a happy return to his land of birth, where son James was also born. As her husband became engrossed in the challenge of developing a strong educational and research base at BUMC, Mrs. Grant turned her energies to learning about the social and political history of the Chinese people and, above all, to a study of the clothing worn by members of the Manchu-dominated Chinese court during the Qing period. Her enthusiasm for the subject and a small inheritance from her father soon led her to collect these opulent costumes.

Reminiscing about her childhood in Beijing, Betty Grant Austin remembered going shopping with her mother in the family rickshaw. As shopkeepers became aware of Mrs. Grant's interest in acquiring the treasured possessions which impoverished members of the deposed Manchu court were forced to sell, they saved fine pieces especially for her. One of her favorite shops was Mr. Dai's, where the back room was reserved for her to view the objects and make her selections. Merchants who came to the Grant residence, Mrs. Austin recalled, resembled Santa Clauses as they traipsed across the courtyard, bags full of wares slung over their backs. "I think it was very lucky that people like mother cared for and preserved these beautiful robes for us to enjoy. Through them we can glimpse what life must have been like so many years ago at the Manchu court," said Mrs. Austin.

James Grant, who was raised in a house filled with Chinese treasures, describes his mother as "a creative person." Much of the furniture he and his wife, Ethel, cherish was designed by Mrs. Grant and is a reflection of her unerring eye for beauty. Grant suggests his mother's collecting activities were aided by his father's status, which enabled the Grants to mix with former members of the court, including Princess Der Ling, who was most helpful in guiding Mrs. Grant to knowledgeable contacts.

Manchu influence on Chinese costume is easily recognizable in the various robes in the collection. The free-flowing robes of the Ming dynasty were not practical for the Manchu, who added vents at the front and back to facilitate mounting and riding horses. Slightly flared cuffs on narrowed-down sleeves allowed more maneuverability when riding and hunting. Ultimately, these northern conquerors incorporated into their functional costumes the beautiful silks and embroideries for which the Chinese had been noted for centuries. The Manchu sumptuary laws of 1759 codified specific colors for clothing to designate rank and official position.

Qing costumes can often be dated according to the style and placement

---

Official's surcoat with mandarin square indicating second civilian rank, 1875-1900. Silk. 1977.199

Overleaf: Woman's unofficial, informal summer robe and coat, 1900-1905. Silk gauze. 1977.209, 1977.214

On brief excursions of four or five days, Empress Dowager Cixi traveled with at least 50 gowns. This robe would have been a favorite, as she had a penchant for pale blue. The robe is decorated with the commonly used script character *shou,* which, combined with the swastika, stands for "ten thousand times long life." Another symbol of longevity, the bat, was also an emblem of happiness. According to Mrs. Grant, the coat once belonged to Cixi. Although the fabric is the gold color reserved for imperial use, the decorative bands are in a color considered more flattering by the empress dowager, who felt that gold did not enhance her complexion.

of decorative motifs. At the beginning of the dynasty, fierce dragons adorned the shoulders and central portions of official robes. When Manchu coats became belted, a smaller, less ferocious dragon motif was positioned on either side of the front both above and below the waist. In the 19th century, robes were decorated with systematically placed Buddhist and Daoist symbols. The symbolic representation of sea and land at the lower border changed from curving diagonal bands topped by turbulent waves and rugged mountains to almost straight lines surmounted by tightly stylized versions of surf and peaks.

The Grant Collection boasts an extensive selection of mandarin squares, badges worn to indicate official status. Squares bearing appropriate bird motifs denoted civil offices while animal symbols designated military rank. Such badges came in sets of two; one to be worn at the center back of the robe, the other at the front. Women displayed the rank of their fathers, husbands, or sons. With their profusion of exquisitely worked silk and metallic threads, the mandarin squares in the Grant Collection maintain a uniformly high standard of workmanship which does not reflect

Empress Dowager Cixi and a royal group in a palace courtyard, Beijing, 1902-1908. Photograph by the court photographer You. Denver Art Museum collection from negative in the collection of Princess Der Ling, Freer Gallery of Art.

the general decline in quality that occurred toward the end of the dynasty.

Pockets obviously fascinated Mrs. Grant, for she acquired more than 200 in various shapes and sizes. These ingeniously fashioned accessories were used to carry such personal objects as eyeglasses, sweetmeats, tobacco, money, earpicks, and fans. Pockets or pouches were customarily given as a gesture of thanks or to honor a festive occasion. They were also a necessity because robes had no pockets.

Decorative components of a robe, like sleevebands, collars, and cuffs, rare in most costume collections, were given major consideration by Mrs. Grant. The sleevebands she acquired include a full range of summer and winter fabrics whose fine designs and impeccable embroidery are a superb testimonial to her taste and acumen as a collector. Most unusual is the representative group of uncut bias cloths showing matched

pieces embroidered to decorate a single robe.

The exhibition also includes some of the unusual, often frivolous, personal possessions of court people. Among them are an emperor's ivory comb, a small bronze handwarmer, silver chopsticks, jade hair ornaments, walnut hand exercisers, and a "devil chaser"—strips of silk interlaced with old Chinese coins which were kept near the bed to ward off evil spirits.

Mrs. Grant not only assembled a fine collection, she also provided an exhaustively annotated inventory of its contents. Her painstaking research and fine documentation have been invaluable and constitute her personal contribution to this catalog and to the exhibition. According to a friend who has been involved with the collection over many years, "There is probably no other assemblage of garments and personal items which has been brought together with the same devotion and the same knowledgeable descriptions as this collection."

Charlotte Hill Grant was devoted to the traditions of Old China and would accept nothing less than superb quality for her collection. To honor her accomplishment, the museum intends to acquire objects which will further complement and enhance the Grant Collection whenever possible. Private gifts and financial support will be essential to the realization of this goal.

Imelda Gatton DeGraw

Woman's unofficial, informal summer coat,
c. 1900. Silk embroidery on silk gauze.
1977.212

Green, which the Chinese considered a shade
of blue, was associated with spring. Single
peony blossoms were frequent embroidery
motifs: the flower symbolized riches and
honor and conveyed hopes for advancement.

Sleeveband (detail), c. 1875. Silk embroidery
on silk satin. 1977.446.1

This embroidered figure—most likely a
representation of Laolang shen, guardian
deity of actors—illustrates ways in which the
Manchu integrated their traditional clothing
with native Chinese styles. The deity wears a
Manchu fur jacket over his Chinese robe. His
sable hat, also of Manchu origin, bears a
sapphire button denoting attainment of the
third civilian rank.

THE MAGNIFICENT MANCHU

In May 1644, fierce Manchu horsemen swept down across the Great Wall to take Beijing from the rebel peasant army which had driven the last Ming emperor to suicide. Under the dynastic name of Qing, they remained to rule all China until the collapse of the imperial system brought about by the revolution of 1911. When they arrived on the Chinese scene, the Manchu were already accomplished bureaucrats with an effective military organization, not the horde of wild, illiterate tribesmen they are usually pictured as being. As a minority ethnic group with its own customs and traditions ruling over 150 million Chinese, the Manchu asserted their cultural identity by imposing on the Qing court their hairstyle and costume: they replaced the flowing, cumbersome robes and flamboyant, upturned slippers of the Ming with boots, trousers, and coats derived from their riding clothes. The Qing dynasty brought little beyond the magnificent Manchu costume style to China, whose cultural traditions remained basically unchanged.

The Manchu were originally known as the Jürchen, a confederacy of Tungusic horse-riding tribes living in Liaodong, now southern Manchuria. The descendants of hunting, fishing, and stock-breeding tribes of

Hanging scroll (detail) showing a Manchu high official on a hunt, probably Qianlong period (1736-1795). Ink and color on silk. Gift of Dr. Robert Rinden. 1970.51

the forest, they had developed an agricultural way of life. Their earlier emphasis on pig raising precluded a nomadic, herding heritage like that of their steppe neighbors, the Mongols. Pigs do not herd. The Jürchen spoke a Tungusic dialect, which, along with Mongolian and Turkish, belongs to the Ural-Altaic language group. Their ancestors had ruled north China as the Jin (gold) dynasty from 1115 until their conquest by the Mongols in 1234. After their defeat, remnants of the Jürchen-Jin returned to their homelands on the middle Sungari River, where they reverted to their previous tribal lifestyle. Then, in the 15th century, they migrated south to the easterly side of the Changbai mountains. A century later, their great leader, Nurhaci, initiated a Jürchen renaissance, which culminated ultimately in their reoccupation of north China.

Nurhaci was born in 1559 into the aristocratic Aisin Gioro clan of the Jianzhou, a Jürchen group living north of the Yalu river. He began his career as a petty feudal chieftan in 1582, when his father and grandfather were killed simultaneously in local tribal warfare. Nurhaci instigated a series of intertribal bloodfeuds and political negotiations until he had managed to unite all the scattered Jürchen into a vast confederacy under one rule. He judiciously maintained ties with the Ming through 1609 and periodically sent tribute

missions, some of which he led himself, to the court at Beijing. The last rival Jürchen tribe to fall was the Yehe; whose chieftan chose to burn with his castle. His dying curse that Nurhaci's clan would someday be destroyed by a Yehe woman resulted in their virtual exclusion from the imperial Qing harem. Among the exceptions was Cixi, the last ruler of China, whose reactionary, autocratic rule contributed to the downfall of the Qing dynasty which the Aisin Gioro clan had established.

Proving himself shrewd and capable, Nurhaci combined his tribal fighting strength with all he could learn of Chinese ways. Because the Jürchen-Jin writing system had been abandoned by the 16th century, he commissioned a new system based on the adaptation of the Mongolian script to Jürchen. The translations he ordered made from the Confucian classics and from Liao, Jin, and Yuan history texts gave him an insight into Chinese ethical and political principles, as well as an opportunity to learn why these three previous barbarian dynasties had failed in their attempts to rule China.

In 1601, Nurhaci began to organize the Jürchen into a powerful military machine under the so-called "banner system," which served as a transition from the feudal past to the bureaucratic organization they fell heir to as rulers of China. All tribesmen, their allies, captives, and slaves were assigned to administrative units named "banners" for the colored flags they flew, each consisting of 300 warriors. In peacetime, these units engaged in fur trapping, the breeding of fine horses, and the cultivation of ginseng, an herbal medicine for prolonging life—all products they traded with the Chinese.

In 1607, Nurhaci declared himself the Sure Kundulen Khan (wise and respected emperor), a title borrowed from his Mongol tributaries. In 1616, he proclaimed himself emperor of the Houjin dynasty. Two years later, he successfully attacked the Ming troops garrisoned in eastern Liaoning province and began his long-planned move toward the conquest of China proper. In the spring of 1625, he shifted his base of operations from his ancestral seat, the fortified town of Hetu Ala, to Mukden (Shenyang), a hundred miles west, originally a Ming town in Liaoning province, which would remain a reservoir of Jürchen-Manchu culture throughout the Qing dynasty. A year later, Nurhaci died in battle, without realizing his dream of conquest.

The Jürchen leadership fell to Nurhaci's eighth son, Hong Taiji, generally known as Abahai, who proved to be a wise and clever statesman. To cement the Jürchen confederacy, Hong Taiji changed the tribal name from Jürchen to Manchu, a term of obscure origin intended to obliterate any association with the tribal past. In 1636, he changed the

Archer's ring, 18th century. Onyx(?). 1977.50
Archer's rings were a traditional part of the Manchu hunter's equipment. Fashioned from a variety of materials, including ivory, jade, and bone, the ring protected the archer's thumb as he drew the bowstring and allowed him to achieve greater distance and accuracy in the arrow's flight. After their conquest of China in 1644, the luxury-loving Manchu used the rings for symbolic rather than practical purposes. Decorative silk cases were especially designed to carry one or two favorite rings.

dynastic name from Houjin to Qing (clear and pure), parodying the Ming (bright), which had become tarnished with corruption. Although he died in 1643 before the conquest of Beijing, as founder of the Qing dynasty, he had already set the stage for this drama. Fearing that his descendants would become victims of sinification, he echoed the emperor Shizong, his 12th century Jürchen-Jin ancestor, in admonishing his people "to follow the old customs in clothing and language, to practice horsemanship and archery regularly so they would be ready for warfare." Consequently, after the Manchu conquest of China, all men, including the Chinese and some foreigners, were required to wear Manchu dress and to braid their hair in a Manchu queue.

Between 1631 and 1638, Hong Taiji designed the basic Qing governmental structure with Confucianism

as the state philosophy. This was a synthesis of Ming bureaucracy and certain Manchu feudal features, including clan cohesion and a court of colonial affairs. The military with its banner system, itself a kind of bureaucracy, continued to be ruled by the emperor and the imperial house, the Aisin Gioro clan. By now, the clan history had been embellished by legends designed to enhance its standing in Chinese eyes. According to these myths, the Manchu culture hero, the first Aisin Gioro, had been conceived in the Changbai mountains after his mother had consumed a red haw berry dropped in her lap by a passing magpie, the clan totem. Unable to care for the infant, she placed him in a birch-bark cradle on the Sungari. Eventually he floated to Sanxing where he was discovered by three clan leaders fighting for supremacy. They immediately declared him Aisin Gioro, meaning gold, and hailed him as their chieftan. Nurhaci and Hong Taiji were his descendants.

Hong Taiji was succeeded in 1643 by his son, Shunzhi, who, though still a child, ascended the Manchu throne in Liaodong under the protection of the regent Dorgon, Nurhaci's fourteenth son. By 1644, there were 278 Manchu, 120 Mongol, and 165 Chinese banners, swelled by deserters, under Dorgon's command. Meanwhile, in China, the Ming were on the verge of losing the "mandate of heaven" because of their corrupt court system and their oppression of the provinces. Their capital was in the hands of the peasant general Li Zicheng. At the invitation of the Ming commander Wu Sangui, who sought them as allies against the rebel forces, the Manchu, under Dorgon, poured into China. On June 6, Dorgon performed the kowtow (three kneelings and nine head-knockings) to heaven, assumed the mandate to rule, announced that he had rescued Beijing, and established the Qing dynasty in China, although it took another forty years to secure the south.

In 1661, Emperor Shunzhi died, and Kangxi ascended the dragon throne as a seven year old under the watchful eye of the Oboi regency until it was dismissed in 1669. During Kangxi's brilliant reign, which lasted until 1722, the southern part of China was finally brought under Manchu rule. Although Kangxi was brought up in the Forbidden City with Confucian ideals, he remained loyal to the traditions of his ancestors. Manchu fashions permeated his court, which displayed a curious mixture of Chinese dignity and barbaric splendor. The Jesuit Matteo Ripa, described Kangxi on their first meeting as "seated crosslegged in Manchu fashion on a divan." Later, he noted that His Majesty slept naked, like a barbarian chieftan, between his fur-lined mattress and quilt. During

Pair of sleevebands (detail), Qing dynasty (1644-1912). Silk. 1977.452.1,2

Kangxi's reign, periodic hunting expeditions to the wild Liaodong terrain of his ancestors were court extravaganzas which involved masses of people and the transportation of three months' provisions.

The Manchu cleverly patronized the Jesuits more for their knowledge of science and the cannon than for their religion, to which they never truly succumbed. The Manchu had originally practiced shamanism, in which the pig was the most important sacrificial beast. In the Forbidden City, after the Manchu conquest, a shaman pole surmounted by a pig bone traditionally stood outside the Kunning gong, the ceremonial palace used for consumating the emperor's marriage. Through contact with their Mongol vassals, the Manchu had also acquired Tibetan Lamaism, a nominally Buddhist, syncretic religion which contained enough animism to appeal to their shamanistic heritage.

The most famous Qing emperor, Qianlong, succeeded Kangxi's son Yongzheng and ruled from 1736 until 1795. This was a period of peace, prosperity, and expansion. China, a

Mandarin square, early 19th century. Silk tapestry. 1977.229

Symbolism abounds in this square, whose golden pheasant identified a second-rank civilian. Growing from rocks on either side of the bird are a peony shrub, a sacred fungus, a lily, and a peach tree. Five bats represent the five virtues: long life, wealth, peace, love of virtue, and a happy end.

vast Manchu showpiece, controlled Mongolia, Chinese Turkestan, and Tibet, while enjoying a brisk trade with the Japanese, Indians, Arabs, Portuguese, Dutch, and English. In 18th century Europe, China was known as the "Celestial Empire." Unfortunately, Qianlong was followed by a succession of weak rulers during a century of turmoil. The increasing Confucianism of the court had stagnated into a moribund tradition afraid of change. Internal unrest and foreign encroachment, including the infamous Opium War, ultimately eroded the empire. Under the stifling hand of Empress Dowager Cixi (1835-1908), all hope of reform or innovation died. With the revolution of 1911, the Qing dynasty and the imperial system ceased to be.

Beyond the cut of their fabulous dress, Manchu contributions to Qing culture are few. The Manchu did not permeate Chinese social life but remained isolated at the court or in their garrisons. Life in the Forbidden City was far removed from that of the Chinese scholar, which seemed weak and effeminate to the Manchu, who prized courage and efficiency. The Chinese literati class revered small jade animals of infinite subtlety while the court doted on grandiose objects like gem-adorned jade boulders. The opulent taste of the court was eclectic and pretentious. The pleasure pavilions designed by the Italian Jesuit Giuseppe Castiglione for the Summer Palace were in the

Italian baroque style while the French Jesuit Benoit based his design for the fountains on Versailles. The Summer Palace in Jehol was modeled after the great Lamasery in Potala. Qianlong even collected western clocks. His choice of an artist to chronicle his military victories over the Mongols of Central Asia was Castiglione, who produced a set of engravings in the European manner.

The Manchu were great patrons of the arts, rather than creators. At the direction of Kangxi, some thirty factories were set up in the Forbidden City to produce traditional objects of metal, lacquer, jade, and ivory in a

style which had reached an overripe maturity by Qianlong's time and which became excessively unpleasant by the end of the dynasty. Manchu court taste can be detected in certain overly ornate ceramic wares decorated with stiff floral motifs on a rich color background, which is always white in traditional Chinese wares. Embroidery styles have been suggested as a source for both color scheme and design.

Painting, on the other hand, with the exception of portraiture, was left to the Chinese literati, who continued the traditions of the Ming and earlier dynasties. The Qing was a great antiquarian age in which huge anthologies, encyclopedias, and large collections of books, paintings, porcelains, and archaic bronzes were published. Secular novels, short stories, and dramas were also extremely popular. The finest was the *Hong Lou Meng (The Dream of the Red Chamber),* the famous 18th century novel by Cao Xueqin which questioned the tyranny of arranged marriages and prophetically foreshadowed the downfall of the old order two centuries later. Having assimilated many elements of Chinese culture in order to rule successfully, the Manchu made no significant contribution of their own to the fine arts, but they did leave a costume legacy which still remains to dazzle the world.

Emma C. Bunker

21

LIFE IN THE FORBIDDEN CITY

During the last years of the Qing dynasty, the Manchu lost more than the mandate to rule: all of China lost a way of life. A series of disastrous events forced the Manchu to deal simultaneously with foreign imperialism and with internal rebellion that forecast the disintegration of Chinese political power, philosophies, and traditions. Only the Forbidden City, the compound in Beijing that housed the imperial family, seemed immune. There court life and customs continued in much the same way they had for centuries. Eunuchs still fawned, court women still sought the emperor's favor, and empress dowagers still vied for power over the empire itself.

To ensure the birth of sons who would perpetuate the imperial family and perform the rites of ancestor worship that were the cornerstone of Chinese society, polygamy was accepted, and there were many concubines at court. To avoid doubts about the legitimacy of their sons, the women were waited on by a large staff of eunuchs, and, with the exception of the emperor, any male found in the Forbidden City after nightfall was tortured or put to death.

Because of the opportunities for advancement and financial gain, many young Chinese men, both married and unmarried, sought to become court eunuchs. They did so despite the fact that only half the candidates survived the primitive operation and despite the belief that

"leaving the family" (as the Chinese euphemistically described castration) made men's bodies and spirits incomplete and, therefore, unworthy of appearing before their ancestors after death. At court, however, a eunuch could advance through 48 different grades and ranks—the higher the rank, the closer his association with the monarch and the greater his opportunity to grow rich through bribery, blackmail, and outright theft. The appeal of this life is demonstrated by the fact that at the height of the Manchu regime, the eunuch population had swelled to well over 6,000. Although eunuchs had been part of the Chinese imperial court since antiquity, their major periods of power often coincided with a dynastic downfall like the overthrow of the Ming. Thus, when the Manchu conquered China in 1644, they found it necessary to limit both the number and the activities of the eunuchs. As the Manchu established control, however, they turned more and more to Chinese ways and became increasingly dependent on the eunuch system.

The eunuchs' penchant for pilfering certainly did not result from inadequate pay. A eunuch received an initial five ounces of silver and was paid a starting salary of one ounce of silver a month, a rate that increased annually. He was also provided with additional funds in time of need: for example, to pay for the funeral of a parent or other relative.

Nor did eunuchs have to worry about their own funeral expenses: the palace paid the bill and maintained a cemetery just for them.

Chinese officials were aware of the demoralizing effect eunuchs had on their system of government, and the "eyes and ears of the officials," court-appointed censors whose job it was to investigate any wrong-doing, issued reports criticizing the eunuchs and their scheming ways and calling them "past-masters of every adroit flattery." Although the eunuchs were, in principle, supervised by the Imperial Household Department, there were actually few restraints on their power.

When they were not conniving to amass great wealth or engaging in other court intrigue, the eunuchs carried out their official duty—supervising and tending to the needs of the ladies of the court. Wearing their sumptuous silk gowns and fluttering their ivory fans, these women—servants, ladies-in-waiting, concubines, and empresses—contributed much to the splendor of the Qing court.

Servant girls were selected from the ranks of Manchu soldiers'

Empress Dowager Cixi and the imperial eunuchs, Beijing, 1902-1908. Photograph by the court photographer You. Denver Art Museum collection from negative in the collection of Princess Der Ling, Freer Gallery of Art.

At front right is Li Lianying, Cixi's chief palace eunuch, who is said to have amassed a fortune of well over two million dollars.

daughters, and the ladies-in-waiting were the daughters of officials. These two groups of women were permitted to leave the Forbidden City after a specified period of service to the court. But concubines and empresses were considered part of the imperial family and were allowed to leave the palace grounds only on special occasions—to journey to the Summer Palace or, in very rare instances, to visit their own homes.

As potential mothers of imperial heirs, concubines occupied a position of respect and were selected from the daughters of Manchu bannermen. Every three years eligible girls from 12 to 15 presented themselves to the Imperial Household Department, which singled out those whose personalities, family ties, and wealth proved satisfactory. The final choice was made not by the emperor but by his mother, the empress dowager, for whom these women would be constant companions. She indicated her choice of a new concubine by dropping a blue silk handkerchief at her feet.

Although the emperor had little say about the selection of the court ladies, he did decide who would share his bed. The names of all the ladies in the imperial family were engraved on jade pieces kept on the emperor's bed table. The "son of heaven" selected a worldly partner by turning one of the small jade tablets face down. A eunuch would dash off to notify the "appointed one" and present her with a yellow brocade cloth in which to wrap herself after disrobing. The eunuch then hoisted her to his shoulders and delivered her with all haste to the emperor's bed. This procedure evolved to hinder assassination attempts since it was believed that "a nude woman carries no weapon except one." The day and hour of the visit were carefully recorded to confirm the legitimacy of any child the woman might bear.

Since he had seventy women to choose from, not all of his concubines caught the emperor's attention regularly. His occasional bed partners were doomed to lonely lives as well-fed, well-clothed prisoners. Longing for family and former friends, such women passed days, weeks, and years waiting on the empress dowager, strolling through the palace gardens, and contemplating how different life might have been. Even the empress was resigned to "eating vinegar" if her husband preferred the company of another woman.

The selection of an empress was no small matter, but it was an affair of state rather than of the heart. A woman—usually older than the emperor—was chosen from a Manchu family of power and prestige to form an alliance equitable for both sides. The empress was the first wife of the monarch and, as such, performed official duties.

The only woman who had more power than the empress was the empress dowager, the emperor's mother. The ideal of filial piety afforded her enormous power over her son and, through him, the empire itself. An empress dowager was not necessarily of noble birth. Even low-ranking concubines could attain the powerful position if they had borne the reigning emperor. And during the last years of the Qing dynasty, one woman, Cixi, did just that. A cunning intelligence and good common sense helped propel Cixi from concubine to empress dowager and made her the real ruler of China for more than fifty years.

When the young Cixi anxiously waited for the blue silk handkerchief to be dropped at her feet, she probably did not envision the dramatic turn her life would take. Fatherless from the age of three, Cixi was forced to rely on the charity of more prosperous relatives. Still, from all accounts, her childhood was a pleasant one, and she was schooled in Confucian classics, art, and literature as befitted her rank.

During the carefree days of her youth, Cixi formed an alliance with a distant male cousin, Rong Lu, who was to remain a constant companion and source of strength throughout her life. It has often been speculated that the two were lovers, a relationship that would have disqualified the girl from being an imperial concubine. The speculation remains just that, but it is interesting to note that

Cixi reportedly wore two jade bracelets the day she presented herself at the palace to be examined by midwives under the close supervision of eunuchs. She emerged minus the two bracelets but with her virginity confirmed and with permission to participate in the final concubine selection.

At the time of her selection, Cixi was designated a concubine of the third rank. She quickly charmed her mother-in-law, and soon Emperor Xianfeng himself took notice. In time, Cixi gave birth to the ruler's only son and thereby became the empress dowager, a position shortly assured by the death of the emperor. At 24, Cixi assumed the reins of command along with Cian, the empress and first wife of the emperor. Thus, two women were to rule China as regents for two children: first, Cixi's son, Emperor Tongzhi, and then her nephew, Emperor Guangxu.

Because Cixi left the rearing of her son largely to eunuchs, he was an indulged and spoiled young man when he assumed the throne at 17. But Tongzhi was not destined to rule long. Within six months, he contracted smallpox and died, leaving a wife, Aleute, with child.

Had Aleute given birth to a son, she would have become the empress dowager. But to assure her own position and power, Cixi ignored imperial custom and appointed another child emperor—her sister's son, Guangxu. His appointment and Cixi's role at

Money bag, 19th century. Silk embroidery on silk. 1977.396

Members of the court considered money transactions degrading and left the responsibility of carrying cash to the head eunuch. The tassels and draw cords of this bag are imperial yellow, indicating it probably belonged to either the emperor or the empress. An emblem of love and affection, the peony became a symbol of feminine beauty when it was placed in conjunction with a flying bat.

court might have been challenged save for the fact that the pregnant Aleute conveniently "mounted the dragon" (died). Cixi's power was consolidated a few years later by the equally suspicious death of Empress Cian, who apparently made the mistake of eating cakes sent to her by her coregent.

Installed as sovereign at 19, Guangxu assumed the outward signs of office but continued, at first, to consult his aunt before issuing important edicts. The young emperor, however, had been tutored in western thought, and during his reign he came under the influence of a young

Chinese liberal bent on reforming the government. The outcome, some ten years after Guangxu assumed power, was the Hundred Days of 1898. During this period, the emperor issued more than 40 reform edicts concerning such things as the modernization of education, the elimination of government bureaucracy, and a restructuring of the tax system that would force the wealthy, rather than the poor, to pay the bulk of taxes.

The edicts were issued without the knowledge of the empress dowager and certainly without her consent, for the "old Buddha" liked things just the way they were. Because her sex had prevented her following more traditional paths of power, she had forged her own route, built on graft, greed, and corruption—just the things the young emperor wanted abolished. After a brief power struggle, Cixi, still vigorous at 63, forced her nephew into retirement and again assumed the regency. She kept that position until her death ten years later.

Cixi died as she had lived, a law unto herself. Conveniently her death came one day after that of Guangxu, thus assuring the old dowager the right to appoint the future emperor. She selected another child ruler, Xuantong, grandson of her lifelong friend and reputed lover, Rong Lu. Thus ended her 50-year rule over a third of the world's population.

Julie Segraves

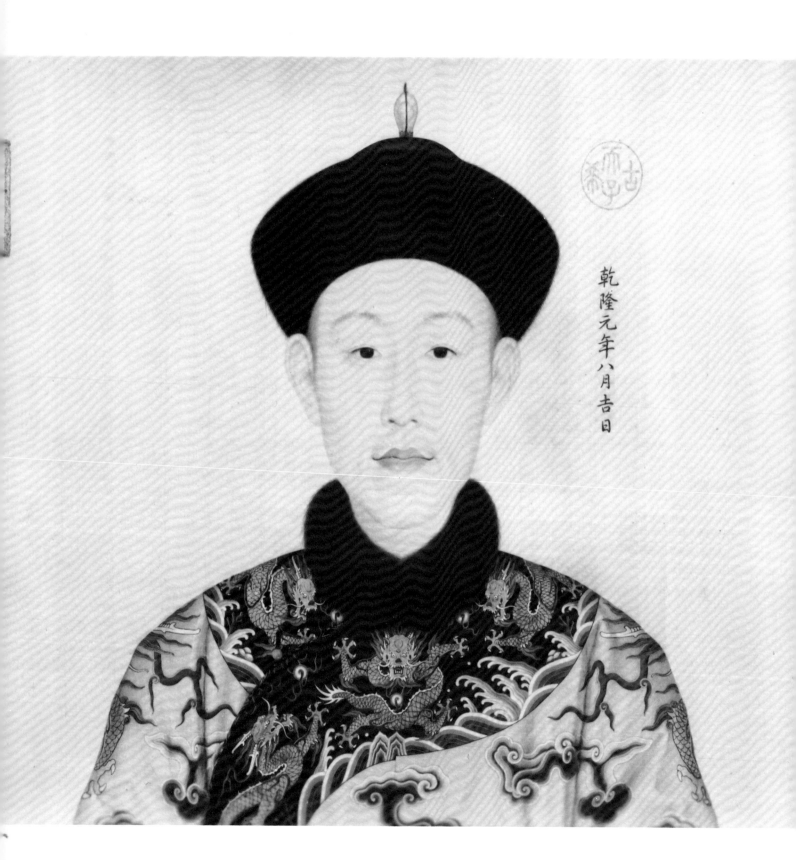

乾隆元年八月吉日

PALACES, PORTRAITS, AND PORCELAINS

The dragon robes, official garments, ecclesiastical vestments, and theatrical costumes of the imperial court are but part of the magnificent legacy of the Qing dynasty (1644-1912). They offer a dazzling glimpse into the sumptuous and elegant life that surrounded the throne of China's Manchu leaders, who had descended from the North and established their dynastic rule over the country. The ancient forms and techniques of Chinese art and architecture captivated these Manchu emperors. They embraced Chinese traditions and did their best to preserve them as their own. With an admiring eye for the past, they built palaces in Beijing, "posed" for formal portraits, and patronized imperial porcelain factories, just as the Chinese emperors of the Ming dynasty (1368-1644) had done.

The rainbow-colored garments of the Qing period were worn in palaces furnished with porcelains, jades, lacquers, cloisonné, and ivories. Artists painted meticulous portraits of the Manchu court wearing rich robes whose color and pattern indicate rank and status. These portrait paintings, in which the court nobles and their ladies sit silently with eyes gaz-

ing straight ahead, convey great faith in the traditions borrowed from China's long history. The centuries of Qing rule, however, brought changes never encountered by previous dynasties. Resolute devotion to past traditions was powerless against the relentless pressures of a new age of global modernization.

By the time the Qing dynasty fell, western-style buildings stood on Chinese soil, built by foreigners and their Chinese imitators. Taking advantage of new technology, Empress Dowager Cixi (1835-1908) had commissioned sober photographic portraits of herself. Traditional porcelains were being copied, not out of an antiquarian love for the past, but as calculated imitations to deceive foreign collectors. Although the confidence of the Qing rulers in the validity of Chinese historical precedent remained steadfast throughout their reign, it was necessarily tempered by the profound transformation overtaking China.

Like their Ming Chinese predecessors, the Manchu used Beijing as their imperial capital. Preserving the appearance of the city, they embarked upon an ambitious architectural program of erecting, restoring, and reconstructing buildings. As prescribed in Zhou (1027-256 BC) ritual books, the Imperial City was situated at approximately the center of the capital. The quadrangular Forbidden City, in turn, sat at the heart of the Imperial City, a rectangular palace

enclosure with walled precincts, tower gateways, marbled courtyards, and majestic halls. Incorporating monumental areas for state audiences, along with private living quarters for the emperor, his family, and staff, the Forbidden City is dominated by deep red buildings with gleaming yellow roofs and polychromed eaves. The colorful buildings provide a vibrant contrast to the white terraces on which they stand.

Aligned on a grand axis from south to north are the Forbidden City's Three Great Halls: Taihe dian (Supreme Harmony Hall), Zhonghe dian (Middle Harmony Hall), and Baohe dian (Protecting Harmony Hall). The sanctity of this three-part scheme is derived from Zhou rituals which attest that the "son of heaven" (the emperor) must rule from three courts.

The first and largest of these halls was used on such solemn occasions as the celebration of New Year's Day, the winter solstice, and the emperor's birthday. Here the ruler sat enthroned before mass audiences while court musicians played stone chimes and golden bells. Behind this first hall was the smaller middle hall, a square building used by the emperor as a waiting area while he prepared himself for ceremonies to be conducted in the Supreme Harmony Hall. The Middle Harmony Hall was also used once a year for the emperor's symbolic examination of agricultural implements and seeds for the new planting, as well as for the preparation of memorial service messages to be read in the Temple of the Ancestors. In the third of the Great Halls, banquets were given to honor ambassadors and vassal princes. Here, too, the emperor received subjects who had earned the highest awards in administrative examinations.

Beyond the walls of the Imperial City in the southern quarter of Beijing stands the Qinian dian (Hall of Annual Prayers). Constructed at the end of the 19th century in the precinct of the Altar of Heaven, it represents the final flowering of Qing ceremonial architecture. Its richly painted woodwork, deep blue roof tiles, and marble terraces, however, belie the changes that China had undergone since the dynasty began. The Hall of Annual Prayers arose in "a world so altered that its largest timbers could be best supplied from Oregon" because China's own lumber supplies had been depleted (Laurence Sickman and Alexander Soper, *The Art and Architecture of China,* 3d ed. [Baltimore: Penguin Books, 1968], p. 288).

In addition to its governmental and ceremonial buildings, Beijing is a city with imperial pleasure palaces, lakes, and hillocks. Emperor Kangxi (reigned 1662-1722) designated an area northeast of the capital for an extensive summer palace. It was enlarged and improved by later emperors, including Qianlong (reigned 1736-1795), who had pleasure pavilions designed by the Jesuit missionary Guiseppe Castiglione (1688-1766) in 18th century Italian baroque style. Ornamented with fountains patterned after Versailles, these extraordinary buildings were furnished with mirrored halls, Gobelin tapestries, and furniture copied from French engravings.

Looted and destroyed by the Franco-British allies in 1860, Castiglione's pavilions now lie in ruin, but the New Summer Palace of Empress Dowager Cixi has survived. It was built northwest of Beijing as her retreat upon retirement in 1889. Remarkably picturesque in its combination of architecture and gardens, this miniature palace city includes halls for state functions, imperial residences, temples, theaters, offices, and guardhouses. Its hillside towers, lakeside pavilions, and arched marble bridges made it the empress dowager's favorite palace. A marble water pavilion in the shape of a large boat still stands a few feet from the lakeshore. Ironically, Cixi was severely criticized for building her extravagant Summer Palace with publicly subscribed funds intended to build a naval fleet—ships that probably would have been destroyed by the Japanese in the war of 1895.

Castiglione, the priest who designed Qianlong's baroque-style pleasure pavilions, is remembered primarily as a painter. Born in Milan,

he entered the Society of Jesus in 1707 and was trained to paint religious subjects. Toward the end of the Kangxi era, he went to Beijing, where he offered his services to the emperor and adopted the Chinese name by which he is known as a painter, Lang Shining. His works combine European perspective and chiaroscuro with traditional Chinese painting methods.

In 1736, Emperor Qianlong commissioned Castiglione to paint his inaugural portrait with his empress and consorts. This painting, now in the Cleveland Museum of Art, depicts the sitters in frontal poses against a neutral ground, as in conventional Chinese ancestor portraits. The emperor's face, however, is rendered with subtle highlights and shadows that reveal Castiglione's European background. The masterful brushwork in Qianlong's robes of imperial yellow and his red velvet cap captures the nuances of silk brocade, fur, and a baroque pearl. Qianlong gave the painting the title: *A Mind Picture of a Well-Governed and Tranquil Reign* (Sherman E. Lee, "Varieties of Portraiture in Chinese and Japanese Art," *Bulletin of the Cleveland Museum of Art* 64 [April 1977]: 118-136). Castiglione's painting is a horizontal handscroll, a rather unusual format for imperial portraits. Typically, such paintings are vertical

Dish with the Eight Buddhist Emblems, China, Qing dynasty, 19th century. Porcelain with overglaze enamels, 18 1/8 in. dia. Anonymous gift. 1974.53

hanging scrolls and, occasionally, album leaves. Most likely, the traditional hierarchy of format was dictated by the use of imperial portraits in ancestral temples, where imposing and impressive images were required. Hanging scrolls were best suited for such situations while handscrolls and albums were appropriate for personal and private viewings.

Executed in precise, meticulous brushwork, traditional portraits were regarded by the literati artists of the Qing dynasty as mere craft and not as part of the artistic mainstream. While frequently mechanical and dry, these portraits are capable of evoking the calculated majesty and magnificence of orderly rule. Typically, such a painting depicted the imperial sitter as a nearly symmetrical, enthroned figure with lavish garments, jewelry, and emblems of power. The clouds, waves, and dragons with flaming pearls of woven and embroidered images are transformed into multi-colored painted patterns.

During the Qing dynasty, an intense antiquarian interest led merchants, scholars, and emperors to amass extensive libraries and collections of art. Painting, calligraphy, poetry, and the other arts flourished. Toward the end of his second decade of rule, Emperor Kangxi established workshops in the Imperial City for the production of lacquer, metal, and enamel wares, as well as glass, furniture, ivory, and jade. Throughout the remaining years of Manchu rule,

these studios produced objects of superb technical quality exclusively for court use.

Attempts to produce porcelains at a conveniently located Beijing workshop were abandoned, however, in favor of the long-established, but distantly located, ceramic manufacturing area of Jingde Zhen. The imperial kilns there were destroyed at the time of Wu Sanguan's rebellion in 1675, but they were subsequently rebuilt and continued to produce porcelains of unmatched quality into the middle of the 18th century. Through experimentation, traditional methods of ceramic decoration were refined, and a rich palette of monochromatic and polychromatic wares was developed. Chinese and western enthusiasts have categorized these porcelains with a sumptuous vocabulary of terms referring to colors and techniques: ox-blood, peachbloom, mirror black, tea-dust, flambé, clair de lune, famille verte, robin's egg, and lacework—just to name a few.

By the end of the Qing dynasty, the general quality of porcelains had declined, and activity at the imperial kilns came to a total halt in 1835 when Taiping rebels destroyed the Jingde Zhen factories. In little more than a decade, sufficient funds were procured to rebuild the imperial potteries, and porcelains of admirable workmanship appeared even in the twilight years of Qing patronage. Since the copying of earlier ceramics was seen as a sign of

vitality, Empress Dowager Cixi sent Qianlong period pieces from her Beijing palace to be copied at the imperial porcelain factories. She also ordered special wares to be made for the Chuxiu Palace, which was constructed at her command for her exclusive use. A large dish in the Denver Art Museum's collection bears the rare base mark of Cixi's private hall, "Chuxiugong zhi," (H. A. Van Oort, *Chinese Porcelain of the 19th and 20th Centuries* [Lochem: Uitgeverstmaatschappij De Tijdstroom B.V., 1977], pp. 54-56). Decorated with colored enamels depicting floral motifs and the Eight Buddhist Emblems, this porcelain plate has the opulent appearance appropriate to its imperial setting.

After the Manchu swept into China in the mid-17th century and established their dynastic domination of the vast country, they assumed responsibility as the imperial protectors and perpetuators of Chinese art and culture. They were blessed, as well as burdened, by the centuries of Chinese tradition which they inherited. Complete assimilation with the Chinese proved impossible, but the Manchu fostering of court art and architecture stands as a testimony to their energetic and determined willingness to heed China's cultural mandate. Imperial robes and portraits and beautiful palaces and porcelains attest to their achievements.

Ronald Y. Otsuka

The Temple of Heaven, Beijing, 1911-1915. Photographer unknown. Reprinted by permission from *Imperial China: Photographs 1850-1912* with historical texts by Clark Worswick and Jonathan Spence (New York: Pennwick Publishing, Inc., 1978).

Ancestor portrait of sixth-rank military official, late 19th century. Ink and colors on paper, 42 x 27 in. framed. Anonymous loan.

KINGFISHER ORNAMENTS

In China, the tiny kingfisher was once prized for its feathers of bright, iridescent shades of blue. As early as the Han dynasty (206 BC-AD 220), bedcoverings and wall hangings were made from the diminutive bird's plumage. During the Tang dynasty (618-906), the feathers were inlaid in gold jewelry worn exclusively at court. In the 18th and 19th centuries, the brilliant feathers were used in large headdresses, oversized earrings, and hair ornaments worn only by the highest ranking court women. To create these shimmering objects, ornaments representing birds, animals, insects, leaves, and flowers were intricately fashioned from kingfisher feathers, Beijing glass, and precious and semiprecious stones. Mounted on gold wire springs and attached to a woven filigree base, they quivered as the wearer moved. At the end of the 19th century, kingfisher hairpins, combs, and other baubles in art nouveau designs began to be produced in great quantity for the domestic market and export to Europe. Ornaments that had once been a luxury now became affordable to all Chinese women, and the increased demand soon led to the extinction of the brightly hued little bird.

Earrings, 19th century. Gold, enamel, and kingfisher feathers. 1977.662

Perforated fretwork tiara (detail), 19th century. Papier-mâché and kingfisher feathers. Charles Bayly Jr. Collection by exchange. 1954.22

JADE HAIR ORNAMENTS

Jade was the most precious of stones to the Chinese. Occurring in two forms, jadeite and nephrite, this hard, translucent mineral is extremely difficult to work and takes a high polish. It was frequently used for personal items like belt buckles and the hair ornaments worn by both men and women. The most elaborate ornaments were reserved for the emperor and his entourage. The pieces on loan from James P. Grant are white, the preferred color, and various shades of green, a color that occurs when iron is present in the stone. The intricacy of the filigree work indicates that these ornaments probably date from the Qianlong period (1736-1795), when some of the most exquisite jade pieces were produced. Reign marks were first used to identify jade objects during this time.

White jade hair ornaments, Qianlong period (1736-1795). Lent by James P. Grant

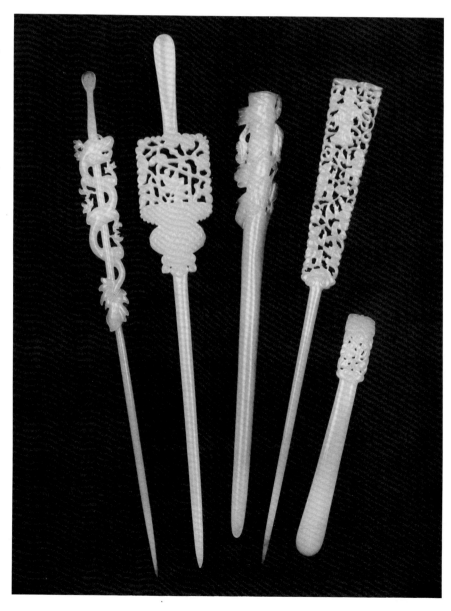

CLOISSONE

Three silver cloisoné boxes. Lent by Betty Grant Austin.

Opium box, late 18th/early 19th century. Motifs from the Hundred Antiques theme cover the body of this box. Budding Fragrance symbols, a *ruyi* scepter, and flowers adorn the lid.

Box, mid-18th century. The knob on the lid of this melon-shaped box is in the form of a peach, the emblem of marriage and a symbol of longevity and springtime. The floating cloisonné work depicts the Hundred Antiques theme.

Makeup box, late 18th/early 19th century. Enameled images of gentlemen's requisites, flowers, and vases decorate the sides of this fluted silver box. On the lid, four wish-granting fairy bats fly beneath a large bat carrying coins, a symbol of prosperity.

The technique of cloisonné was probably introduced into China from the West during the Yuan dynasty (1260-1368). It was during Qianlong's reign (1736-1795) in the Qing dynasty, however, that production reached its peak. In the cloisonné procedure, the cloisons (wires) are shaped before being soldered onto the vessel; then colored enamels are applied between the wires, and the piece is fired. The small boxes on loan from Betty Grant Austin's collection were designed to carry such personal items as makeup, opium, toothpicks, or perfume.

Overleaf: Woman's vest, before 1850. Silk. 1977.216

Dynastic statutes established the appropriate seasons for the court to wear different types of fabric. The thin silk or gauze garments reserved for summer wear are exemplified by this sleeveless vest, which a court lady could wear for unofficial, informal occasions. The lotus plant, which is the dominant decorative motif, was the Chinese emblem of summer and fruitfulness.

Woman's informal robe, late 19th century. Silk damask. 1977.203

Although damask was produced in China prior to the invention of the drawloom, its manufacture was neither efficient nor economical. The single-color, reversible cloth of this robe is representative of fabrics woven on a drawloom with a single set of warp and weft threads. Medallions with two lions (Dogs of Fu) playing with a ball are evenly spaced over the robe. Because lions were believed by Buddhists to be defenders of the Law and protectors of sacred buildings, their purpose here may have been to guard the wearer of the robe.

Album leaf (detail) from a series of 18 rice paper paintings describing the methods of cultivating, preparing, and weaving cotton (Qing dynasty, 1800-1850). Bibliothèque Nationale, Paris (B.N. Oe 97). Reproduced by permission from *Cotton and Silk Making in Manchu China*, ed. Laura Casalis and Gianni Guadalupi (New York: Rizzoli International Publications, Inc., 1980), pl. vii. The spindle-wheel initially used for silk spooling was adapted for use in reeling cotton.

Album leaf (detail) from a series of 23 colored engravings illustrating the breeding of silkworms and the working of raw silk (Qing dynasty, 1800-1850). National Library, Florence (Banco Rari 76). Reproduced by permission from *Cotton and Silk Making in Manchu China*, pl. xiv. The raw silk is unwound from cocoons onto a reel.

SILK TECHNOLOGY IN ANCIENT AND MEDIEVAL CHINA

By the beginning of the Ming dynasty (1368), China possessed a fully developed textile technology able to produce materials of superb quality. Of these, the most highly prized was silk, a material of good tensile strength, light in weight, easy to dye, and suitable for summer and winter use. Its desirability gave it economic importance and made it the best-known fiber material in premodern times. Both the fabrics and the textile technology of China were transmitted to the West over the famous Silk Road. To manufacture their exquisite silks, the Chinese had perfected the art of silkworm cultivation and developed sophisticated devices for reeling, spinning, and weaving silk fibers. Introduced into Europe during the first millennium AD, these machines had a profound influence on textile production in medieval Europe.

By the third millennium BC, the Chinese were producing silk from both wild silkworms (*Rondotia menciana* Moore) and domesticated silkworms (*Bombyx mori* L.). The earliest evidence for *R. menciana* Moore is the artificially cut half cocoon excavated in 1926 in Shanxi province. Fragments of silk cloth from the reeled silk of *B. mori* L. were discovered in 1958 in Zhejiang province. To date, they are the earliest finds of silk in China.

Wild silkworms supplied the fluffy wadding for padded garments and quilts; threads from wild cocoons were best suited for embroidery. Domesticated silkworms produced the finest quality silk, and their cultivation was, and is, a serious business on which the Chinese over the centuries have written many treatises. The caterpillars which hatch from the eggs of *B. mori* L. are initially reared in basket trays on a diet of chopped mulberry leaves. As the caterpillars mature, they are transferred to straw cocks where they spin their cocoons. Certain caterpillars are allowed to progress through the chrysalis stage and emerge from the cocoons as moths, which lay eggs for future generations of silk producers. Today in China five generations of silkworms are reared from May to October. In most instances, however, to ensure the "endless" threads required for fine silks, the moths are killed just before they emerge, and the fibers are unwound from the intact cocoons onto reels. The fineness of the silk depends on the number of cocoon fibers combined to form a single thread in the reeling process, which produces continuous threads from 700 to 1600 meters long.

The earliest reeling devices were hand driven, but, by the Northern Song period (960-1126), an efficient and economical method of reeling silk by a treadle-operated machine had been invented, probably in the northern Chinese province of Shandong. This machine was not surpassed in either China or Europe until the invention of the steam-powered reeling machine in the 19th century (Dieter Kuhn, "Silk Technology in the Sung Period (960-1278 A.D.)," *T'oung Pao* [1981]).

Another Chinese invention was the spindle-wheel. Developed in historic times from a Neolithic-period hand spindle, the spindle-wheel was initially used for silk spooling, the further processing of silk thread through transfer from a reel to a spindle and thence to a bobbin. In later times, the spindle-wheel was used for doubling and quilling, the twisting together of two or more silk threads.

Overleaf: Woman's informal outer coat, c. 1850. Silk embroidery on wool. 1977.201

Although the fabric of this coat closely resembles felt, it is a plain-weave brushed wool. Motifs symbolizing endurance, happiness, long life, beauty, and refinement are embroidered in satin stitch. The red color implies that the coat was worn on a happy occasion.

Woman's unofficial coat, c. 1900. Silk tapestry. 1977.207

Chinese craftsmen perfected the tapestry technique of using a needle as a shuttle, which allowed the weaver to achieve extreme subtlety of color and design. By the Qing dynasty, tapestry-weave fabrics (*kesi*) were so highly coveted for court robes that their use outside the court was restricted. Chrysanthemums, a symbol of fall and endurance, and butterflies, representing long life, form the decorative medallions on this robe, whose plum color signifies winter. Formal robes were sometimes worn for an unofficial occasion, which, in this instance, may have been the Chrysanthemum Festival, celebrated on the ninth day of the ninth month.

Album leaf (detail) from a series of engravings. National Library, Florence (Banco Rari 76). Reproduced by permission from *Cotton and Silk Making in Manchu China*, pl. xx. The drawloom shown here required two operators: the drawboy, who controlled the lifting of the warp threads to create complex designs, and the weaver, who attended to the batten and picking.

Left: Uncut bias bands, c. 1875. Silk embroidery on silk. 1977.492

After a silk fabric was woven, it was usually sent to the imperial workshops where skilled craftspeople followed cut-paper designs to embroider the cloth for court use. Court robe accessory sets included eleven bias bands and a collar, which were cut to form the decorative borders of the sleeves, closure, and neckline of the robe. The size of these bands indicates that they were designed for a jacket.

Overleaf: Uncut bias bands (detail), c. 1875. Silk embroidery on silk. 1977.492

Apron, c. 1875. Silk embroidery on silk satin. Gift of the Hubert W. Keith Estate. 1969.28

Eventually, the doubling and quilling process was applied to plant fiber yarns, as well as silk thread. This led finally to spinning yarn directly on the spindle-wheel, a technique which contributed to a three-fold increase in productivity. The spindle-wheel was probably introduced into Europe by the second half of the first millennium AD, and, although it did not allow for continuous spinning, it remained the only labor- and time-saving device for spinning thread until the invention in 15th century Europe of the spinning wheel with flyer, an apparatus which made continuous spinning possible (Dieter Kuhn, "The Spindle-wheel: A Chou Chinese Invention," *Early China*, no. 5 [1979-80]).

Loom technology developed along with spinning technology. High standards of production and specialized workshops which produced a large variety of silk fabrics were already in existence by about 1300 BC when the Shang kings established their capital near Anyang (Dieter Kuhn, "The Silk-workshops of the Shang Dynasty (16th-11th Century B.C.)," *Jubilee Volume in Honour of Dr. Joseph Needham* [Shanghai, 1981]). Perhaps the most delicate fabric manufactured was damask (*qi*), which was woven on a horizontal loom consisting of a warp beam, a cloth beam, and pattern rods. Since the pattern rods had to be hand lifted, the loom dictated a preference for monochromatic, geometric designs.

About the 5th century BC, the invention of a treadle-operated loom led to increased production of silk fabrics and mastery of polychrome weaving. Most notable were brocades in many new designs. Finds from the tomb of Lady Dai indicate that textile production and craftsmanship had reached a high point by the beginning of the Han dynasty in the 2nd century BC. Although the treadle-operated loom of the Han dynasty was the most advanced of its period, it lacked the versatility of the drawloom, which made economically feasible the production of complexly patterned fabrics on a large scale. The drawloom, which required two people to operate, may have been invented in China between the Han and Tang dynasties, but Persian or Syrian origin is also possible. During the Tang dynasty (618-906), Chinese weavers abandoned the warp-patterning method in favor of Sassanian weft patterning.

Dieter Kuhn

Uncut sleevebands (detail), c. 1890. Silk and metallic embroidery on silk satin. 1977.479

Sleeveband (detail), c. 1825. Silk embroidery on silk gauze. 1977.477.1

Because the *fangsheng* lozenge forming the overall design of this band is a widely used Confucian fertility symbol, it is appropriate for a woman's costume.

Overleaf: Man's topcoat (back), c. 1900. Silk tapestry. 1977.208

The "stone black" color of this formal coat was worn by princes of the first and second degree and other male members of the court who had not been sanctioned by the emperor to wear yellow. Within the medallions, dragons are surrounded by blue-green clouds sprinkled with red bats and Buddhist symbols. The sleeves appear to have been shortened.

Woman's dragon robe (detail), 1875-1900. Silk tapestry. 1977.198

This robe illustrates the changes that had occurred in dragon robe decoration by the end of the Qing dynasty. The once-bold dragons were reduced in size and ferocity, good-luck symbols became stylized, and clouds became tightly clustered over a background diaper pattern. On earlier robes, tall peaks rose above swirling waves; here, squat mountains rest on stiff, slanting stripes representing water. Although the robe is now faded, its original hue may have been a grayed violet favored by Empress Dowager Cixi.

MANCHU STYLE AND ETHNIC IDENTITY

Clothing is one of the most consistent forms of cultural expression. Through its clothing, a society creates images that communicate group identity and often reflect the evolution and development of the culture itself. These images contribute to notions of style that are used to differentiate one group from others. The two major costume styles that survive from the last dynastic period of China are evidence of the fact that during the Qing dynasty, the Han Chinese were ruled by the Manchu, an alien group from the north. Linguistic and cultural differences separated Manchu from Chinese; but costume style, particularly in the outer garments exposed to public view, conveyed these ethnic distinctions and gave each group a sense of identity.

Chinese and Manchu styles shared many elements. Cultural borrowing from the Chinese by the Tungus-speaking Manchu began in the 14th century, and by the 17th century the two cultures shared a single source for the raw materials used in clothes making, a common repertoire of ornament, and a respect for the role clothing played in social organization and control. In spite of these similarities, the Manchu style preserved a set of visual signals directly linked with a cultural memory. It was in part defined by a specific set of structural characteristics—tapered sleeves, flared cuffs, curved front flaps, skirt vents, loop-and-toggle fastenings—which reflected a discrete set of re-

sources among the garment-making traditions of eastern Asia. These characteristics, as well as the way in which garments were worn or decorated, conveyed messages connoting an ethnically distinct style.

Morphologically, Manchu garments were more closely related to the animal-skin clothing of nomads from the southern Siberian forests than to the cloth garments produced by the Han people of the Chinese plains. Although all surviving Manchu garments are made of cloth, construction features like angled shoulder seams, the emphatic curve of the front flap closing on the extreme right side, and the trapezoidal profile of Manchu coats derive from animal-skin prototypes. Details like the loop-and-toggle fastenings underscore cultural links with Amur River tribes whom the Manchu acknowledged as ancestors and continued to protect from Chinese cultural contamination.

Other costume messages suggest the evolution of the Manchu from forest-dwelling hunters to a mounted-warrior society based on Mongol models. The gender-exclusive clothing that characterized much of the Manchu wardrobe paralleled the segregation of sexes by occupation that occurred in steppe societies. Three-quarter and waist-length coats dominated male attire while women's clothing was usually full length. The adoption of horse riding led to a customized male ward-

robe that included short, vented coats with flared cuffs, trousers, boots, and paired aprons to protect against chafing and wind chill and to meet needs for mobility and portability. Coat skirt vents indicated occupational distinctions: vents at the front and back permitted a male rider to sit astride a horse while vents coinciding with side seams accommodated the forward motion of women walking.

The assimilation of cloth into Manchu garment-making traditions probably occurred during the transition to a mounted-warrior society. Ancestors of the Manchu who occupied the strategic area north of the Liaodong Peninsula maintained

Mandarin square (detail), c. 1875. Silk tapestry. 1977.225.1

The bat was a popular symbol of longevity and happiness.

Overleaf: Summer dragon robe, c. 1750. Silk embroidery on silk gauze. 1977.191

The style and placement of the dragons on this robe are based on the sacrificial nine-dragon robe introduced by Emperor Yongzheng (1723-1736). Large single dragons are embroidered on the front and back of the upper robe, across each sleeve, on either side of the skirt front and back, and on the inner flap below the side closure.

Woman's official, informal robe, c. 1850. Silk embroidery on silk satin. Gift of Mrs. Frederic H. Douglas. 1973.274

This special-occasion robe has embroidered medallions of peonies and butterflies. The Eight Buddhist Emblems are interspersed in the traditional sea patterns surmounting the slanted bands.

51

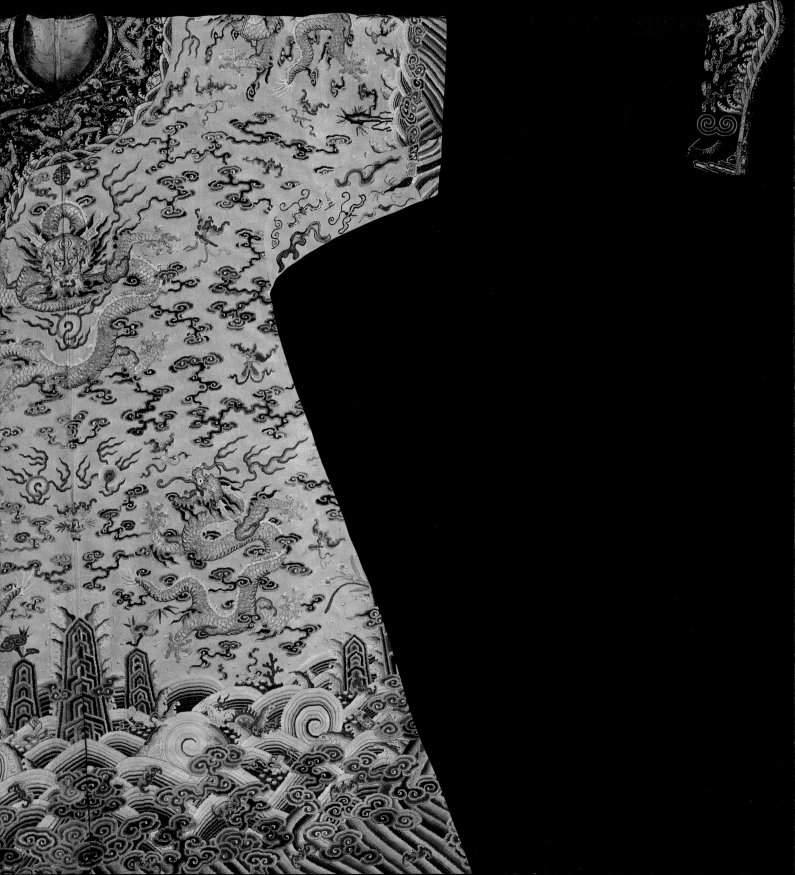

tributary relations with the Chinese court during the 15th and early 16th centuries. In exchange for their submission to imperial authority and the consequent acquisition of trade rights, chieftains were granted titles and the accoutrements of rank, including silk coat yardages. The impact of these gifts of dragon-patterned silks was still evident in the disposition of zones of ornament on 19th century Manchu court coats.

In a Chinese context, Manchu garments became politically significant in the 16th century when the Manchu clans consolidated their power north of the Great Wall and declared their intention to conquer the Chinese empire. After the conquest in 1644, in addition to fostering Manchu identity, Manchu-style clothing became one component of a political program aimed at bolstering the control of a large population by a small group of conquerors. Although the Manchu could claim ethnic superiority in martial terms, they were obliged to acknowledge the primacy of imperial authority and a cultural bias that discriminated against non-Chinese elements; and their clothing came to express notions of political control that were linked to a particular Chinese cosmological view through a specific iconography.

According to Chinese imperial precedent, garments belonged either to the category of official public attire or to the category of unofficial

domestic wear. Official attire was worn by everyone participating in government; hence, during the Manchu period, all public clothing communicated Manchu domination and was strictly regulated by the state. In contrast, unofficial clothing was not formally regulated and preserved the ethnic division between the Chinese and Manchu populations. Costume in either category was graded in three divisions of formality, most clearly marked in official costume, where legislation eventually prescribed the range of clothing and accessories for each officially recognized court rank.

At court, *formal dress* was reserved for specific ritual occasions and was restricted to the highest-ranking officials. *Semiformal dress* was used for all other official court functions. It was worn by anyone of rank conducting official government business. *Informal dress* provided the necessary wardrobe for public events not connected directly with ritual or government. The unofficial costume for both the Manchu and the Chinese was similarly graded.

Coats and auxiliary coats were the main vehicles of cultural expression for Manchu costume. The basic trapezoidal profile was typical of three key garment types: a long-sleeved, cuffed coat with a curved front flap fastened with loops and toggles along the right side; a front-opening surcoat with elbow-length sleeves; and a front-opening sleeveless coat. In various

configurations, these three garments formed a wardrobe that differentiated male from female attire and provided both genders with at least six grades of clothing. Except for the placement of skirt vents, similar full-length coats were worn by both men and women for all but the most formal court rituals. Men's coats were belted while women's coats hung loose from the shoulders. Women's official surcoats were always full length in contrast to the three-quarter length surcoats worn by men. Unofficially, both might use a waist-length surcoat. Sleeveless coats were worn exclusively by women—full-length with official formal attire, and waist- and full-length for informal and semiformal unofficial occasions.

At the time of the conquest, the Manchu did not possess a wardrobe of sufficient size to satisfy the public and private requirements of rulers within the highly structured and regimented contexts of the Chinese empire. Basic Manchu costume consisted of functional clothing worn at all times as occupational costume and auxiliary attire that could be put on over functional garb for ceremonial wear. Preconquest Manchu costume was assigned new functions, but most Manchu-style garments of the Qing period were invented specifically to meet the demand for an expanded wardrobe.

The most conservative of Manchu garments—ceremonial wear—became the most formal court dress. Male

formal attire consisted of a modified coat, surcoat, and pair of aprons that had evolved from the once-functional riding costume of warriors. Female attire consisted of a composite sleeved and sleeveless coat over which was added a second sleeveless coat. Accessories for both sexes included an archaic form of hat with button ornament indicating rank that had evolved from a close-fitting, fur-lined cap and a flared tippet collar resembling the hood collars of some nomadic and riding coats. Shape and structure were the most important features of Manchu formal court attire because they provided links with the past and were symbolically the most removed from Chinese styles. Decoration employed elements of Chinese imperial iconography, but its organization was adapted from the Chinese dragon-patterned coat yardages sent as gifts to the Manchu in the

Empress Dowager Cixi and attendants, Beijing, 1902-1908. Photograph by the court photographer You. Denver Art Museum collection from negative in the collection of Princess Der Ling, Freer Gallery of Art.

Overleaf: Young matron's informal jacket, 1900-1910. Silk damask. 1977.218

Although it was required that Manchu women's unofficial informal clothing retain Manchu-style sleeves and cuffs, Chinese women were allowed to wear traditional Chinese clothing on informal occasions. The deep black satin yoke of this Chinese-style coat is decorated with a reverse appliqué of a lotus plant and bird.

Eyeglass pouches, c. 1875. Silk embroidery on silk. 1977.432, 1977.331.3

15th and 16th centuries.

By far the largest surviving body of costume belongs to the grade of semiformal court wear. The major garment was a long-sleeved, cuffed coat patterned with dragons in a schematic landscape representing the universe. This garment had no preconquest precedents, and its evolution can be traced through the first century of Manchu rule. The full-length coat evoked Manchu style through its structural details; its decoration emphasized the Manchu intention to establish cosmic rule in accordance with the most ancient Chinese practices. Semiformal dress also included a short-sleeved surcoat. Its prime function was to bear the insignia badges indicating court rank. The formal hat, but with a smaller button, was worn with semiformal attire. By the 19th century such practices as wearing the formal collar with semiformal surcoats on both formal and semiformal occasions tended to obscure distinctions of grade.

Components of Manchu occupational costume were adopted for official informal dress, which included specialized riding, traveling, and hunting garments as well as a range of honorific and general purpose garments. The various kinds of

Mandarin square, c. 1850. Silk petit point. 1977.233

The tiger was the emblem of the fourth military rank.

costume in this group are often difficult to identify since there was no unified iconography. Imperial elements, particularly dragons, are often present. They are usually self-patterned, symmetrical arrangements of circular medallions based on formal Chinese conventions. Color and materials were the chief indicators of status and rank. Possibly because of its comparative plainness, little informal attire was acquired for western costume collections.

The distinction between official and unofficial Manchu clothing rests largely in decoration. Although some elements of imperial iconography were used, dragons were noticeably absent from unofficial garments. Differences between the three grades of unofficial dress were usually defined by garment profile and placement of decoration. The more formal coats generally featured flared cuffs, possibly in an exaggerated form, and were decorated with eight symmetrically placed medallions either isolated on the field or above a wave border. Informal coats were characterized by squared-off sleeves, often with ornamental facings turned

back, and decoration scattered uniformly across the field. Combinations of these features produced an indistinctly graded intermediate range of coats. Matching full-length surcoats with eight medallions were formal while waist-length jackets and short or long sleeveless coats were less formal. The same auxiliary garments with front flaps fastened to the right side were informal. The absence of hats and stiff collars also characterizes unofficial wear.

Structural and technical examination of Manchu garments reveals that much of what we identify as Manchu style was created to meet a new range of social and political demands imposed on a warrior society when it assumed the mandate to rule an established empire. By the Qing period, the assimilation of Chinese cultural principles, including costume technology, was so complete that it is impossible to distinguish Manchu from Chinese garments on the basis of raw materials, decorative vocabulary, symbolic intent, or even on the hieratic use of costume. Only at the level of structure and garment shape or profile can we read the messages that reflected the evolution and development of the Manchu culture and asserted Manchu identity as conquerors within Chinese society, whose traditions were otherwise dominant.

John E. Vollmer

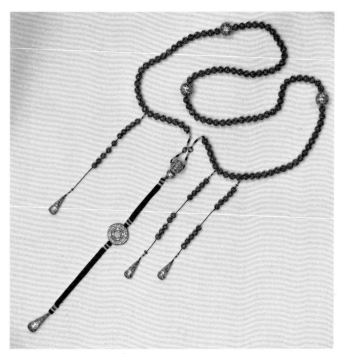

Mandarin chain, c. 1850. Cloissone. 1977.560

The mandarin chain was developed from a Tibetan rosary sent in 1643 by the Dalai Lama to the Manchu ruler. To make the chain uniquely Manchu, a long drop extension, which served as a counterweight to the chain as well as an ornament, was added to the back. Three counting strings were further Manchu embellishments. Dynastic laws and regulations determined the appropriate occasions for wearing these chains and who was entitled to wear them. Materials for the beads were specified according to rank and the particular occasion. Men wore one chain with formal court dress while women were required to wear three; the empress dowager wore a principal chain of eastern pearls with two chains of coral. The chain illustrated here is of the finest cloissoné befitting one of great rank.

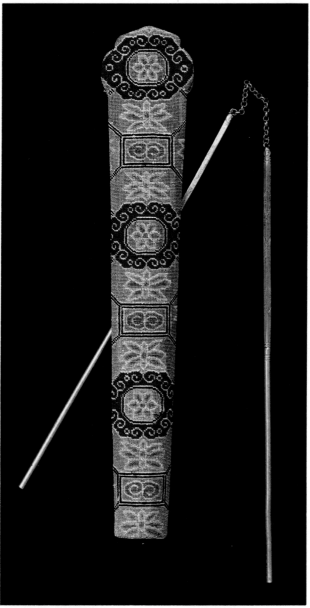

Pocket and chopsticks, c. 1875. Pocket, silk embroidery on silk, 1977.648; chopsticks, silver, 1978.40ab

Woman's semiformal robe, c. 1875. Silk and gold embroidery on silk satin. Lent by the Pan-Asian Collection.

This robe displays the 12 traditional symbols of imperial authority, whose use, according to the 1759 Manchu sumptuary laws, was restricted to formal and semiformal robes of the emperor, empress, and heir-apparent. The symbols were arranged in order of importance in three rings falling at the neck, the waist, and the knees. Regulations further specified that imperial robes be adorned with nine dragons, auspicious clouds, and the Eight Precious Jewels, which symbolized good luck.

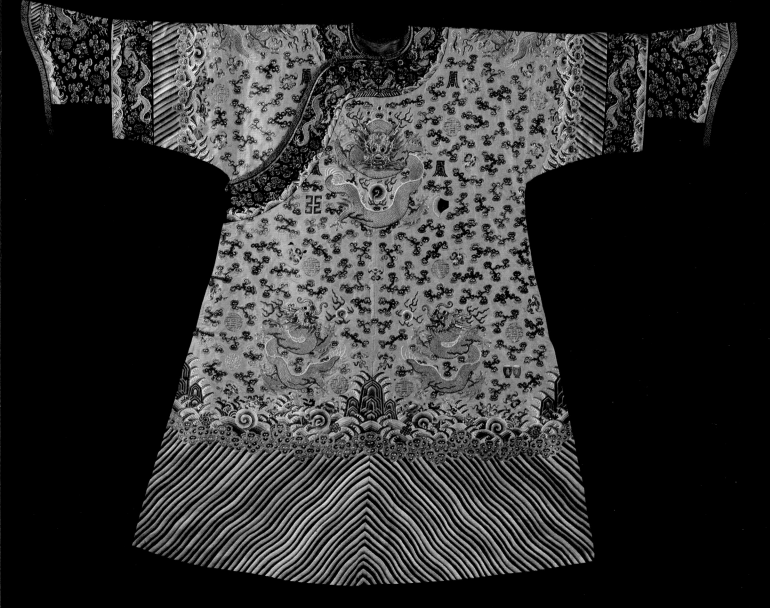

FOOT-BINDING

Scholars disagree about the reason young Chinese women were subjected to the grueling process of foot-binding. According to some, it was initiated a thousand years ago by Yaoniang, a Chinese prince's concubine. Her tiny feet allowed her to walk with such grace that she became known as the "Lily-footed Maiden," and many women chose to have their feet bound to achieve the same grace. Another story records that her lover ordered her feet bound so they looked like new moons, which aroused his erotic desire. Still others say the practice started out of sympathy for an empress with club feet. Possibly the most logical reason is that foot-binding kept one's wife from going astray.

Foot bones were broken and the foot bound to stop growth when girls were between four and eight. Bandages were tightened regularly until the desired shape was achieved, and even then bindings were never permanently removed. As tiny feet became the mark of respectability, women of all social levels participated. In certain regions, a woman with normal feet was considered immoral. So firm was the belief in foot-binding that a betrothal could be broken if a man discovered his bride did not have tiny feet. Earlier edicts forbidding the practice were ignored, and it was not until the 20th century that the custom died out.

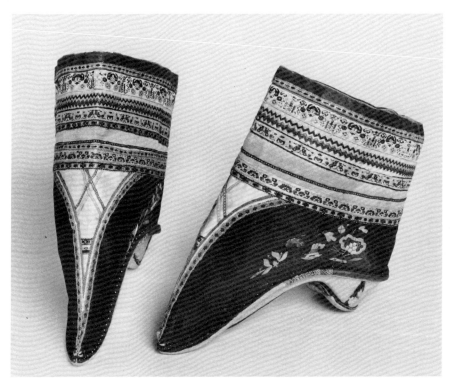

Pair of shoes, c. 1875. Silk embroidery on silk satin. Gift of the Hubert W. Keith Estate. 1969.24ab

The tiny shoes once worn over bandaged feet are covered with delicate motifs embroidered in stitches appropriate to the scale of the shoes. This pair measures 4½ inches from toe to heel.

Mandarin square, c. 1800. Silk embroidery on silk. 1977.251

The mandarin duck designated the seventh civilian rank. Here it stands on blue rocks amid waves filled with wealth symbols, ribboned clouds, bats, and a variety of plants. A couched key-fret border of gold frames the square, which is worked in satin stitch.

Qing Dynasty Mandarin Square Emblems

MANDARIN SQUARES

The Chinese practice of wearing badges to signify rank began during the Yuan dynasty (1260-1368), when China was conquered by the Mongol ruler Kublai Khan, and continued with modifications until the end of the Qing dynasty (1644-1912).

When the Manchu invaded China in 1644, they brought with them their system of indicating official rank by wearing jeweled hat spikes and decorated belt buckles. Because subduing south China took precedence over establishing new clothing regulations, the Manchu continued to enforce Ming sumptuary laws until 1652, when they began to introduce their own clothing laws, including badge regulations. Both Manchu and Chinese members of the Qing government were required to wear outer coats with squares bearing emblems which indicated official status; bird emblems identified civil ranks, animals indicated military ranks. Women wore the emblems of their fathers, husbands, or sons. Although the Manchu based their badge system on that of the Ming dynasty (1368-1644), the changes they made were extensive: squares were smaller, and a sun disk was added to the microcosm of clouds, sea, and rocks which customarily appeared on the squares.

Because the Manchu invasion disrupted silk production, Qing-period squares were at first woven of threads spun from peacock feathers or gold. Embroidery, if any, was worked in simple couching stitch, which made more economical use of scarce silk thread than other stitches. By the reign of Emperor Kangxi (1662-1723), silk production was again thriving, and squares from this period show more lavish use of colored silk thread heavily embroidered on backgrounds and borders. These ostentatious badges became more refined during the Qianlong period (1736-1795), when the most elegant mandarin squares were executed. Worked in satin stitch, they depicted birds or animals perched on weathered crags amid cascading seas. Backgrounds were mostly plain, dark-colored silk, and borders a simple key-fret design.

Good-luck symbols, which appeared frequently in Chinese folk art, did not come into vogue at court until the end of the Ming dynasty, when they began to appear in backgrounds (251). Along with Daoist and Buddhist symbols (229), these good-luck symbols occur in profusion in early 19th century squares. Symbols of various kinds proliferated at such a rate that the birds and animals indicating rank became obscured by decorative elements (243). After the Hundred Days of Reform (1898), the overcrowded decoration of the late 19th century was replaced by a design showing the rank-indicating emblem gazing toward a sun disk, with a simple background of clouds. Any symbols were confined to the borders. Although there was a minor revival of older styles in the early 20th century, the elegance and significance of the mandarin squares died when the Qing dynasty ended. (Based on information in "Chinese Mandarin Squares: Brief Catalog of the Letcher Collection" by Schuyler Cammann, *University of Pennsylvania Museum Bulletin* 17 [June 1953]).

Mandarin square, 1850-1900. Silk petit point. 1977.239.2

Three bats carrying artemisia leaves fly over a Manchurian crane, emblem of the first civilian rank. The leaves were believed to keep evil spirits away.

Mandarin square, c. 1900. Silk embroidery on silk. 1977.240

The golden pheasant designated second civilian rank.

Overleaf: Mandarin square, c. 1850. Silk embroidery on silk. 1977.227

The bear in the center of this square was the emblem of the fifth military rank.

Mandarin square, c. 1840. Silk embroidery on silk. 1977.230

Used to indicate the third and fourth military ranks, the leopard and the tiger bear a greater resemblance to their live counterparts than most animal symbols. In the late Qing period, the leopard's spots look like faint circles while the tiger's stripes are comma-shaped. This square is worked in Pekinese stitch on blue satin.

Mandarin square (detail), c. 1850.
Silk embroidery on silk. 1977.227

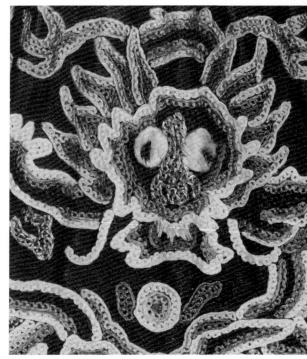

Tobacco pouch (detail), c. 1875.
Silk embroidery on silk. 1977.294

Pocket front (detail), c. 1875.
Silk embroidery on silk. 1977.275

Mandarin square (detail), c. 1875.
Silver and gold thread on silk. 1977.246

CHINESE EMBROIDERY

Chinese silk embroidery first reached the western world in quantity in the late 13th century when Marco Polo and other Italian merchants began to travel the famous Silk Road across Asia. Although Chinese needle-workers have produced thousands of pieces since then, time has taken its toll on these fragile objects, and relatively few examples exist today. Many of them are small pieces—pockets, sleevebands, and mandarin squares. Those in the Grant Collection provide a superb record of the embroiderer's skill and repertoire of stitches, as well as a compendium of traditional designs that reflect the Chinese reverence for the past.

Of special interest are a matching pocket and purse worked almost entirely in trigram stitch, also called "fly stitch" or "hemp stitch" (328.1,2). Chinese embroiderers used this stitch to construct the hexagonal designs which pervade Daoist symbolism. Associated with the tortoise, which represents longevity, endurance, and universal strength, the hexagon itself is made up of triangles formed by this three-sided stitch. It is intriguing to note how many shapes can be built up from these simple geometric figures.

The collection includes excellent examples of Peking knot stitch, illustrated here in a detail from a colorful mandarin square (227). The stitch is similar to the French knot, but the manner of twisting the silk thread creates a different luster and a more precise knot than the French

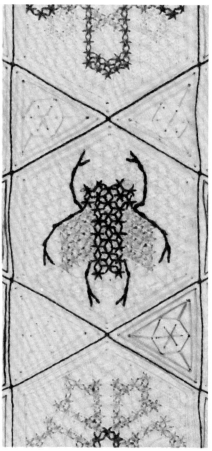

Over-the-belt pocket and matching eyeglass pocket (detail), c. 1875. Silk embroidery on silk satin. 1977.328.1,2

Overleaf: Man's summer dragon robe (detail), 1800-1825. Silk embroidery on silk gauze. 1977.192

Mandarin square, c. 1875. Silver and gold thread on silk. 1977.243

The first military rank was designated by a *Qilin,* the mythical creature depicted in the center of this square.

version. Recent research indicates the Peking knot was sometimes called "Forbidden stitch" because it was once reserved for use on imperial robes worked by embroiderers in Beijing's Forbidden City.

Like Peking knot stitch, Pekinese stitch is also most effective when worked with silk thread. It consists of lines of back stitches laced with circular loops of loose buttonhole stitch. On a handsome drawstring bag in the Grant Collection, coils of gold thread inserted in some of the back stitches add striking accents (294). Worked entirely in Pekinese stitch, a pocket from the collection illustrates how beautifully shaded designs can be achieved with tight rows of small Pekinese stitches (275).

Satin stitch was favored in 19th and 20th century Chinese embroidery. In one exquisite example, the embroiderer has massed flowing rows of satin stitch to create the waves and clouds that surround the central figure (251). Laid flat instead of being twisted, the lustrous strands of silk emphasize the contours of the abstract design. Following the same direction as the long-and-short stitches which make up the shaded areas of the mandarin duck, these smooth satin stitches provide a perfect foil for the raised texture of the figure. Because untwisted flat silk was also used for the long-and-short stitches that model form, their impact depends primarily on subtle color gradations. Many artists dyed their own threads to ensure the range of

tones needed to create the three-dimensional effects which distinguish the finest examples of long-and-short work.

The patience required of a needle artist is particularly evident in embroideries worked in couching, long strands of thread held down by tiny "couching" stitches. The artist can achieve amazing changes of tone by couching gold threads with colored ones. Extraordinary perfection of stitching marks the couched Pearl of Wisdom motif found in a mandarin square from the collection (246).

Because most of it was stitched on a fine canvas of silk mesh gauze, Chinese petit-point work has proved extremely durable. Multiple strands of silk stitched into the canvas produced strong, shimmering surfaces. The mandarin square depicting a fierce tiger (233) has been worked in vertical stitches passed over two rows of canvas threads while the design on a needlepoint pocket (427) has been worked in a traditional diagonal tent stitch.

The Chinese reverence for tradition has preserved the ancient designs used by embroiderers for centuries. Geometric patterns, images from nature, and motifs derived from Daoism and Buddhism have continued to challenge each generation of embroiderers to create masterpieces that combine perfection of technique with beauty of design.

Elsa S. Williams

Pocket (detail), c. 1875. Silk petit point. 1977.427

Left: Mandarin square (detail), c. 1850. Silk petit point. 1977.233

Far left: Mandarin square (detail), c. 1800. Silk embroidery on silk. 1977.251

Overleaf: Woman's informal coat, 19th century. Silk embroidery on silk taffeta. 1977.204

POCKETS

During the latter part of the Qing dynasty, men and women of the court wore separate pockets of various shapes and sizes because Manchu robes were constructed without them. Attached to belts or garment fastenings, they were most commonly used to carry personal articles such as fans, spectacles, and chopsticks. Some unassembled pockets in the Grant Collection indicate that they were made in the same manner as other robe accessories—woven, embroidered, and then sewn together.

Pocket, c. 1875. Silk embroidery on silk. 1977.417

Watch pocket, c. 1875. Silk embroidery on silk. 1977.325

Pocket, c. 1875. Silk embroidery on silk. 1977.392

This pocket probably held a fan, pen, or paint brushes.

Pocket, c. 1875. Silk embroidery on silk.
1977.306

Left: Pocket, c. 1875. Gold and silver
embroidery on silk. 1977.413

Pocket, c. 1875. Silk and gold embroidery on
silk. 1977.424

Fan case, c. 1875. Silk embroidery on silk.
1977.351

Tobacco pouch, c. 1875. Silk embroidery on
silk. 1977.294

BIBLIOGRAPHY

Bland, J. O. P., and Backhouse, E. *China under the Empress Dowager.* London: J. B. Lippincott Company, 1910.

Cammann, Schuyler. *China's Dragon Robes.* New York: Ronald Press Company, 1952.

_____. "Chinese Mandarin Squares: Brief Catalogue of the Letcher Collection." *Bulletin of the University of Pennsylvania Museum* 17 (June 1953).

Dorn, Frank. *The Forbidden City: The Biography of a Palace.* New York: Charles Scribner's Sons, 1970.

Durrant, Stephen. "Sino-Manchu Translations at the Mukden Court." *Journal of the American Oriental Society* 99 (Oct.-Dec. 1979): 653-661.

Kuhn, Dieter. "Silk Technology in the Sung Period (960-1278 A.D.)." *T'oung Pao* (1981).

_____. "The Spindle-wheel: A Chou Chinese Invention." *Early China* 5 (1979-1980).

_____. "The Silk-workshops of the Shang Dynasty (16th-11th Century B.C.)." *Jubilee Volume in Honour of Dr. Joseph Needham.* Shanghai, 1981.

Kwanten, Luc. *Imperial Nomads: A History of Central Asia 500-1500.* Leicester: Leicester University Press, 1979.

Lattimore, Owen. *Inner Asian Frontiers of China.* Boston: Beacon Press, 1962.

Medley, Margaret. *The Chinese Potter: A Practical History of Chinese Ceramics.* New York: Charles Scribner's Sons, 1976.

Michael, Franz. *The Origin of Manchu Rule in China.* New York: Octagon Books, 1972.

Oxnam, Robert B. *Ruling from Horseback.* Chicago and London: University of Chicago Press, 1976.

Sickman, Laurence, and Soper, Alexander. *The Art and Architecture of China.* 3d ed. Baltimore: Penguin Books, 1968.

Siren, Osvald. *The Imperial Palaces of Peking.* 3 vols. Paris and Brussels: G. Van Oest, 1926.

Sullivan, Michael. *The Arts of China.* Rev. ed. Berkeley, Los Angeles, and London: University of California Press, 1977.

Tregear, Mary. "Manchu Taste in Qing Porcelain Decoration." In *Decorative Techniques and Styles in Asian Ceramics,* edited by Margaret Medley. Colloquies on Art and Archaeology in Asia, no. 8. London: University of London, Percival David Foundation of Chinese Art, School of Oriental and African Studies, 1979.

Valenstein, Suzanne G. *A Handbook of Chinese Ceramics.* New York: Metropolitan Museum of Art, 1975.

Vollmer, John E. *Five Colours of the Universe: Symbolism in Clothes and Fabrics of the Ch'ing Dynasty (1644-1911).* Hong Kong: Edmonton Art Gallery, 1980.

_____. *In the Presence of the Dragon Throne: Ch'ing Dynasty Costume (1644-1911) in the Royal Ontario Museum.* Toronto: Royal Ontario Museum, 1977.

Wiethoff, Bodo. *Introduction to Chinese History from Ancient Times to 1912.* Boulder, Colorado: Westview Press, 1975.